AMERICA AT WAR

THE WAR IN AFGHANISTAN
2001–PRESENT

Steve Goldsworthy

MEDIA ENHANCED BOOKS

AV2 BY WEIGL™

ADDED VALUE • AUDIO VISUAL

www.av2books.com

AV² provides enriched content that supplements and complements this book. Weigl's AV² books strive to create inspired learning and engage young minds in a total learning experience.

Your AV² Media Enhanced books come alive with...

Audio
Listen to sections of the book read aloud.

Key Words
Study vocabulary, and complete a matching word activity.

Video
Watch informative video clips.

Quizzes
Test your knowledge.

Go to www.av2books.com, and enter this book's unique code.

Embedded Weblinks
Gain additional information for research.

Slide Show
View images and captions, and prepare a presentation.

BOOK CODE

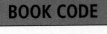

H783109

AV² by Weigl brings you media enhanced books that support active learning.

Try This!
Complete activities and hands-on experiments.

... and much, much more!

Published by AV² by Weigl
350 5th Avenue, 59th Floor
New York, NY 10118

Website: www.av2books.com   www.weigl.com

Library of Congress Control Number: 2013941534

ISBN 978-62127-653-1 (hardcover)
ISBN 978-62127-654-8 (softcover)

Printed in the United States of America in North Mankato, Minnesota
1 2 3 4 5 6 7 8 9 0 17 16 15 14 13

052013
WEP040413

Editor: Heather Kissock
Design: Mandy Christiansen

Photograph Credits
We acknowledge Getty Images, Alamy, and Newscom as our primary photo suppliers. Page 42: Grateful Nation; Page 43: Veterans War Memorial of Texas.

Every reasonable effort has been made to trace ownership and to obtain permission to reprint copyright material. The publishers would be pleased to have any errors or omissions brought to their attention so that they may be corrected in subsequent printings.

CONTENTS

America at War

The United States is a country that was born out of conflict. The American Revolutionary War was a fight for independence from **colonial rule**. From 1775 to 1783, colonists fought British rule for the right to forge their own destiny. Their commitment to the cause established the country as a fierce and loyal **ally**. When called upon, the United States has always fought bravely to protect its values and way of life.

Fighter jets have played a key role in the War in Afghanistan, firing on enemy targets and providing air support for forces on the ground.

Much of the War in Afghanistan is taking place in mountains and other remote areas. Helicopters are considered the best mode of transport for getting troops in and out of these areas.

Since its inception, the United States has been involved in a number of wars and conflicts. These include the War of 1812, the American Civil War, the Mexican-American War, and several battles with American Indians. The United States was also involved in the latter stages of World War I and played a major role in World War II. Since 1945 alone, the United States has taken part in conflicts in Korea, Vietnam, Iraq, and Afghanistan.

No matter how a war ends, it usually leads to changes for both sides of the conflict. On the global scale, borders change, new countries are created, people win their freedom, and **dictators** are deposed. Changes also occur on a national level for almost every country involved.

The United States has experienced great change as a result of war. War has shaped the country's political, economic, and social landscapes, making it the country it is today.

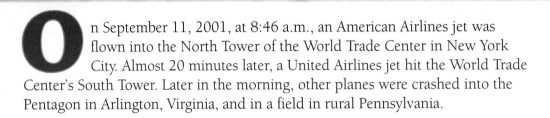

A War Begins

On September 11, 2001, at 8:46 a.m., an American Airlines jet was flown into the North Tower of the World Trade Center in New York City. Almost 20 minutes later, a United Airlines jet hit the World Trade Center's South Tower. Later in the morning, other planes were crashed into the Pentagon in Arlington, Virginia, and in a field in rural Pennsylvania.

By late afternoon, there were strong indications that a militant Islamist group called al-Qaeda, led by Osama bin Laden, was responsible for the attacks. In an address to the nation at the end of the day, President George W. Bush vowed to find the people responsible for these attacks and bring them to justice.

Emotions ran high. While the U.S. government worked to confirm the attacks' instigators, U.S. soldiers prepared to take action. Then, on September 20, President Bush announced his war on terror. Referred to as Operation Enduring Freedom, this war would begin in Afghanistan with al-Qaeda as its main target.

Nearly 3,000 people were killed as a result of the September 11 attacks.

The Roots of the Conflict

SOVIET INVASION

Due to its strategic position between the Middle East, Central Asia, and India, Afghanistan has long been considered a coveted possession. Countries have even gone to war to claim it as their own. In 1979, **Soviet** troops invaded Afghanistan and installed a **communist** government. **Guerrilla** forces called the mujahideen, or "holy warriors," pledged a **jihad** to expel the invaders. After 10 years of fighting, the Soviets pulled out of Afghanistan in 1989. They left a country that did not have a stable government, which set the scene for civil strife.

CIVIL WAR

Civil war has been an ongoing struggle in Afghanistan. After the Soviets withdrew from Afghanistan, the country was unable to maintain a stable government. Afghanistan's defense minister, Ahmad Shah Masoud, tried to broker peace, but his attempts were unsuccessful. The **Taliban** then rose to power. Masoud formed the Northern Alliance to resist the Taliban, and the country lapsed into another civil war. His assassination by al-Qaeda two days before September 11 influenced the U.S. decision to focus its war effort on the Taliban and its al-Qaeda allies.

AL-QAEDA

Created in the late 1980s, al-Qaeda seeks to establish a radical religious and political Islamic state in Muslim countries throughout the world. Al-Qaeda embraces an extremist military view of Islam that is rejected by mainstream Muslims. Members of al-Qaeda are hostile toward any Western culture or world view. Western countries include most of Europe and North America, particularly the United States. To fight the perceived threat from Western countries, al-Qaeda has launched several terrorist attacks on Western countries and their citizens.

THE TALIBAN

The Taliban took control of the Afghan government in the late 1990s. Like al-Qaeda, the Taliban takes an extremist approach to Islam. While in power, the Taliban publicly endorsed Osama bin Laden and al-Qaeda. It even allowed al-Qaeda to set up training camps in the country. When bin Laden apparently masterminded the bombing of U.S. embassies in Africa in 1988, the United States asked that he be deported to stand trial. The Taliban refused. The Taliban then refused a second request after the September 11 (9/11) attacks.

The War on Terror

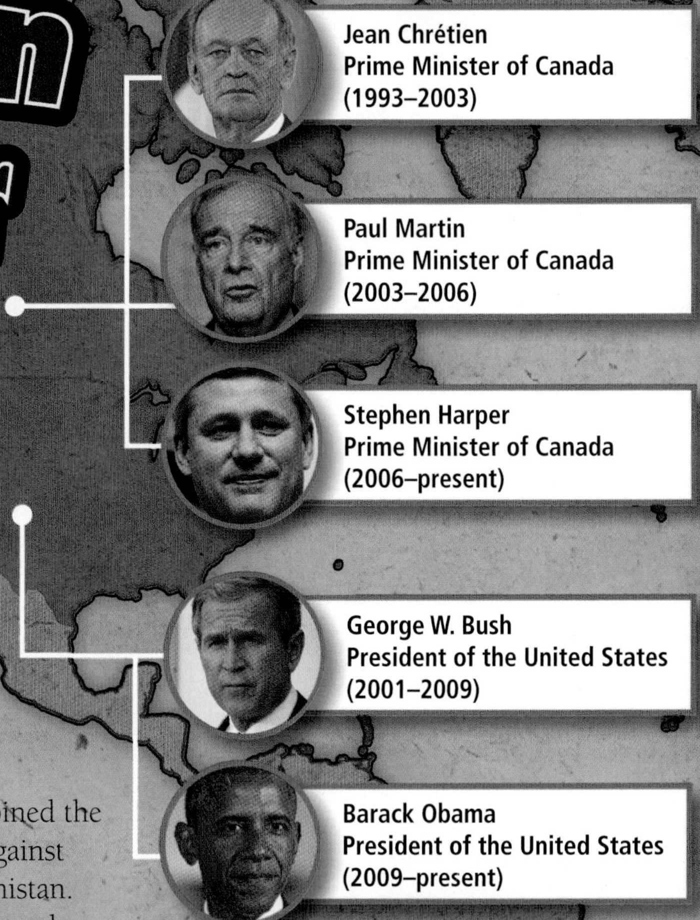

Jean Chrétien
Prime Minister of Canada
(1993–2003)

Paul Martin
Prime Minister of Canada
(2003–2006)

Stephen Harper
Prime Minister of Canada
(2006–present)

George W. Bush
President of the United States
(2001–2009)

Barack Obama
President of the United States
(2009–present)

Almost 50 countries have joined the United States in its fight against **insurgent** forces in Afghanistan. Some joined the United States in the early stages of the war. Others joined in December 2001 as part of a security mission established by the United Nations. The troops involved in this mission are known as the International Security Assistance Force (ISAF). The ISAF has established a strong military presence throughout Afghanistan to help provide stability and security to the people living there.

This map shows the international scope of the war and several leaders who have played key roles in it.

Tony Blair
Prime Minister of the United Kingdom
(1997–2007)

Gordon Brown
Prime Minister of the United Kingdom
(2007–2010)

David Cameron
Prime Minister of the United Kingdom
(2010–present)

Jacques Chirac
President of France
(1995–2007)

Nicolas Sarkozy
President of France
(2007–2012)

Osama bin Laden
Leader of al-Qaeda
(1988–2011)

John Howard
Prime Minister of Australia
(1996–2007)

Mullah Mohammed Omar
Leader of the Taliban
(1994–present)

Kevin Rudd
Prime Minister of Australia
(2007–2010)

Hamid Karzai
President of Afghanistan
(2004–present)

Julia Gillard
Prime Minister of Australia
(2010–present)

Legend

International Security
Assistance Force (ISAF)

Insurgents

Neutral

0   1,000 Miles

2,000 Kilometers

N

The United States Enters the War

With war declared, the United States moved quickly to ready itself for battle. Within days, the United States had secured a coalition force that included troops from the United Kingdom, France, Canada, and Australia. By the end of September, the Central Intelligence Agency (CIA) had a team working covertly in Afghanistan, scouting locations and developing the plan of attack.

By October 7, 2001, U.S. naval ships, including aircraft carriers, had moved into position in the Arabian Sea south of Afghanistan in preparation for the initial attack on the insurgent forces.

The War in Afghanistan began officially on October 7, 2001, with all countries in the coalition focused on the same goals. The Taliban was to be removed from power. Al-Qaeda and Osama bin Laden were to be brought to justice. Terrorist training camps and **infrastructure** in Afghanistan were to be destroyed, and a free and **democratically** elected government was to be established in the country.

The first phase of the October 7 strike came from the sky. U.S.-led airstrikes began attacking airports in key Afghan cities. During the first few days of fighting, U.S. bombers conducted raids on al-Qaeda training camps. In the meantime, U.S. and British navy ships, situated in the Arabian Sea and Persian Gulf, launched Tomahawk cruise missiles on Taliban and al-Qaeda targets. U.S. Army Special Forces groups worked with Northern Alliance troops to wage the ground battle against Taliban forces. They also began the search for Osama bin Laden among the caves and tunnels of the Tora Bora Mountains.

By late October, U.S. fighter bombers began to break through the Taliban front lines. Finally, on November 13, Northern Alliance troops took possession of Kabul, Afghanistan's capital city, and ousted the Taliban from power. The first significant victory was won, but the War in Afghanistan had only just begun.

George W. Bush
The 43rd U.S. President

George Walker Bush was born in New Haven, Connecticut, on July 6, 1946. He is the eldest son of Barbara and George H. W. Bush, the 41st president of the United States. George W. Bush graduated from Yale University in 1968, and Harvard Business School in 1975. Prior to entering politics, he was a successful businessman, working in the oil industry. He began his political career with an unsuccessful run for a seat in the House of Representatives. In 1994, however, he was elected the 46th governor of Texas.

Six years later, George W. Bush was elected the 43rd president of the United States. His election campaign focused on increasing military spending, cutting taxes, and improving education. President Bush faced the first big challenge of his presidency eight months into his first term, when the terrorist attacks of September 11, 2001, occurred. National security became the focus of his presidency. Besides committing the country's military to the war on terror, he created the Department of Homeland Security, a Cabinet department whose purpose is to protect the United States and its territories from terrorist attacks. He also ordered sweeping changes to the U.S. military. George W. Bush was re-elected as president in 2004 and served until January 2009, having completed his second term.

In 1989, George W. Bush became a part-owner of the Texas Rangers baseball team. Even though the team was later sold, he remains a Rangers fan.

President Bush and his wife Laura have two daughters, Jenna and Barbara. The daughters are now adults, but the family remains close.

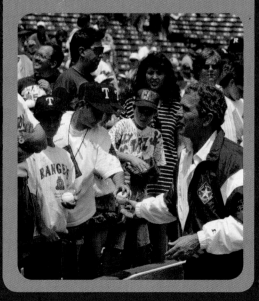

Timeline

The War Overseas

March 1 to 18, 2002
Coalition forces join the U.S. military for Operation Anaconda, a 17-day battle in the Shah-i-Kot valley of eastern Afghanistan.

October 7, 2001
U.S. troops begin combat operations in Afghanistan alongside Afghan troops.

November 13, 2001
With help from U.S. Special Forces, Northern Alliance troops enter Kabul and rid the city of the Taliban.

The War at Home

September 20, 2001
Following the 9/11 terrorist attacks, President Bush addresses the nation and announces the War on Terror.

July 13, 2008
Taliban soldiers attack a small U.S. outpost along the Pakistan border in the Battle of Wanat.

July 2 to August 20, 2009
Operation Khanjar takes place in the Helmand River valley, a Taliban stronghold.

June 2011
President Obama announces a plan for combat troop withdrawal from Afghanistan by the end of 2014.

November 25, 2002
The Department of Homeland Security is formed.

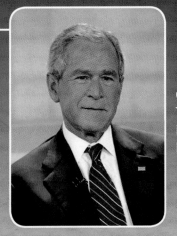

October 26, 2001
The USA PATRIOT Act is signed into law by President Bush.

Americans Serving in Afghanistan

When President Bush declared the War on Terror, troops from all branches of the armed forces began to prepare for the overseas mission. Within weeks, U.S. troops were in position to begin the battle against the terrorist forces in Afghanistan.

From its onset, the War in Afghanistan has required a variety of skill sets. Traditional military divisions, such as the army and the air force, have played an integral role in locating and decimating enemy positions. They have been supported and, in some cases, led by Special Operations divisions. Special Ops troops are trained to handle unique military missions and advanced technology. This combination of traditional and cutting-edge skills and equipment has made the U.S. military a formidable force on the battlefields of Afghanistan.

Infantry

The infantry of the United States Armed Forces are the foot soldiers who fight on the ground during war. They are engaged in face-to-face combat with the enemy. Infantry soldiers possess a solid knowledge of weapons, shooting positions, and personal movement. They are also lethal in hand-to-hand combat situations.

Infantry troops had to be specially trained to handle the extreme weather of Afghanistan. Besides patrolling the mountains and caves of rural Afghanistan, they have also had to fight their way through inner-city environments, moving building-to-building in search of enemy fighters.

Airborne divisions are just one of the infantry contingents fighting in Afghanistan. Airborne troops are trained in air assault techniques.

Marines

The United States Marine Corps combines the mobility of the U.S. Navy with the tactics of the U.S. Army. They are an **amphibious** unit, working in both water and land environments. They work closely with the U.S. Navy for transportation and **logistics**.

Newly enlisted Marines are put through an intense 12 weeks of boot camp. They learn basic infantry skills as well as additional Marine Combat Training. This includes a special Marine Corps Martial Arts course.

The marines are especially suited for fighting in isolated and tough conditions, far away from U.S. security. When the War in Afghanistan began, the 15th and 26th Marine Expeditionary Units were among the first regular U.S. forces to set foot in the country.

Some women Marines are assigned to Female Engagement Teams in Afghanistan. These groups conduct patrols and work with Afghan women to build trust and provide aid.

SPECIAL FORCES

The first U.S. military unit on the ground at the beginning of the War in Afghanistan was the 5th Special Forces Group. Special Forces Groups are also known as the Green Berets, due to the color and style of their headwear. Special Forces soldiers are experts at unconventional warfare, **reconnaissance**, and counter-terrorism. Their skill set was invaluable to the initial stages of the War in Afghanistan. The Green Berets accompanied the advance CIA group into the country in early October. They then gave strategic and military guidance to the Northern Alliance troops in their fight against the Taliban.

Sailors

With more than 317,000 active personnel, the United States has the largest navy in the world. It operates 283 ships, including 62 destroyers and 11 aircraft carriers, as well as more than 3,700 aircraft.

The Navy played an important role in the initial strike against enemy forces in Afghanistan in 2001. Shortly after war was declared, ships were ordered to the area. Once in position, U.S. Navy destroyers and cruisers launched dozens of long-range missiles at key Afghan locations. These attacks were supplemented by fighter jets that took off from U.S. Navy aircraft carriers, carrying out deadly raids and fact-finding missions.

Crewmembers prepare the ship for battle by moving missiles and other weapons into place before the fighting begins.

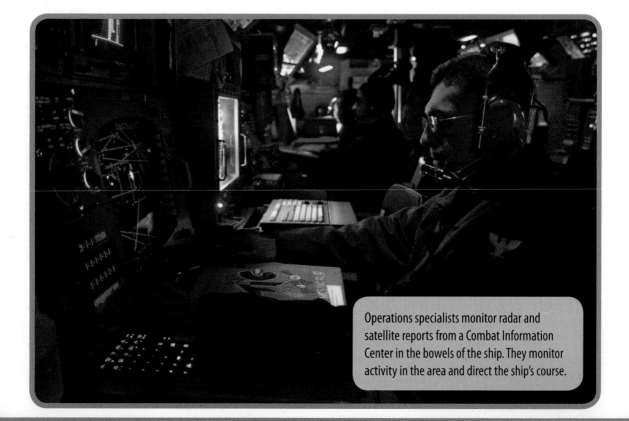

Operations specialists monitor radar and satellite reports from a Combat Information Center in the bowels of the ship. They monitor activity in the area and direct the ship's course.

Pilots

U.S. military pilots were among the first soldiers to engage in combat in Afghanistan. They participated in strategic bombing of targets and ground attacks on the enemy. Some pilots operated bombers at high altitudes, striking Taliban training camps and military targets. Other pilots launched their aircraft from U.S. aircraft carriers in the North Arabian Sea, flying F/A-Hornet fighter-bombers. Many pilots operated specially equipped helicopters, such as the Apache attack helicopter.

Pilots often carry troops to combat zones and offer air coverage in battle. Some fly secretive reconnaissance missions, collecting information on enemy movement as well as locations of enemy bases and camps.

The U.S. Air Force has established bases in strategic locations throughout Afghanistan. The base at Bagram is home to Thunderbolt attack aircraft. Pilots of these jets go on daily missions around the base to monitor enemy activity and provide high-altitude cover to ground forces.

A Soldier's Uniform

Soldiers in Afghanistan have to be prepared for the environment in which they are fighting. This means having the proper battle gear as well as appropriate clothing for the surroundings. Afghanistan can be hot or cold, depending on the time of year and the location. The U.S. military took steps to ensure that its troops were prepared for this challenging environment.

HEADGEAR

When heading into combat, the main headgear for a soldier in Afghanistan is the Advanced Combat Helmet. Covered with a cloth camouflage cover, the helmet is constructed with **ballistic** fiber such as Kevlar and Twaron. A ballistic Nape Pad can be attached to protect the back of a soldier's neck. Night vision devices can be snapped into the mounting bracket on the front of the helmet. Chin straps keep the helmet snugly in place.

JACKET

The jacket of a soldier's uniform is made from thick, flame-resistant fabric. Designed to camouflage its wearer in the wide-ranging terrain of Afghanistan, the material features seven different shades of beige, green, and brown. Special infrared tabs are sewn into each shoulder. This allows people wearing night-vision devices to identify "friendly" troops in the dark. The front of the jacket is zippered and reinforced with Velcro. Blouse bellows, or special folded segments in the sides of the jacket, allow for increased mobility.

BOOTS

A soldier's combat boots are geared toward the environment. Army combat boots are worn in temperate climates. They stand 8 inches (20 centimeters) high and have tan soles. Mountain combat boots are worn in rough terrain. Much like a sturdy hiking boot, they are constructed from tan leather and have a black toe and black rubber soles.

TROUSERS

Army Combat Uniform trousers are worn with a 2-inch (5-cm) wide nylon belt. There is one storage pocket on each thigh and each calf. There are also two Velcro pouches on the knees where the soldier can insert knee pads. Many combat trousers are made with flame-resistant material.

BODY ARMOR

Soldiers in the field are equipped with an Improved Outer Tactical Vest (IOTV) that protects their body from enemy fire. Its components include a collar, a groin protector, soft armor panel inserts, and four ballistic plate inserts for the front, back, and side. When fully equipped, the vest can weigh 30 pounds (14 kilograms). It also comes with its own system of load-carrying equipment, such as pouches and other accessories. The entire system can be released with the pull of a single cord, allowing wearers to rid themselves of excess weight in an emergency.

CAMELBAK

Soldiers fighting in desert conditions are well aware of the dangers of heat exhaustion. Their strongest defense is drinking plenty of water. Most soldiers use a CamelBak water system to carry their water supply. The CamelBak looks like a small backpack. A tube extends from the water pack to the wearer's mouth, giving the wearer easy access to water when needed.

MOLLE

Soldiers in Afghanistan carry their ammunition and equipment in a system called MOLLE, or Modular Lightweight Load-Carrying Equipment. MOLLE consists of several pouches and rucksacks that can be attached to the IOTV. Individual pieces can be added or removed from the main system as required.

Afghanistan War Weapons

The War in Afghanistan is different from most other wars because terrorists do not follow the rules of war as set out by the United Nations. This means they do not fight in traditional ways. The U.S. military has had to adapt to these conditions using a range of equipment and strategies.

ASSAULT RIFLES

One of the most common guns used in the War in Afghanistan is the M4 Carbine assault rifle. The M4 Carbine has selective fire options. It can shoot in semi-automatic mode, in three-round bursts, and as a fully automatic weapon. First manufactured in 1993 by the Colt Company, it is a popular weapon with the U.S. Marine Corps. Its short, light design allows soldiers better operation in **close quarters combat**.

TOMAHAWK MISSILES

The Tomahawk missile is a long-range cruise missile that was developed by the U.S. military in the 1970s. It is most commonly launched from platforms on marine craft such as destroyers or submarines. The missile is composed of several sections. The top section is the warhead. This is the explosive part of the missile. The Tomahawk is equipped with several sensors and tracking devices that hone in on predetermined targets. These sensors can be over-ridden at anytime by operators, who can then send the missile toward an alternate target.

ATTACK HELICOPTERS

One of the most effective weapons in the War in Afghanistan has been the Boeing AH-64 Apache attack helicopter. The Apache is a four-blade, twin-engine helicopter with a two-man cockpit. It has a nose-mounted target sensor and a night vision system, allowing it to zero in on enemy positions. Onboard weaponry includes missiles, rocket pods, and an M230 Chain Gun. A unique feature of the Apache helicopter is its helmet-mounted display. The movements of the pilot's head are linked with the chain gun so it can shoot wherever the pilot is looking.

FIGHTER BOMBERS

The twin-engine supersonic F/A-18 Hornet fighter jet was one of the first weapons to be used in the War in Afghanistan. The Hornet was originally designed for air battles and ground attacks. It has been used by the U.S. Navy and Marine Corps since the 1980s. The Hornet has a top speed of Mach 1.8. It can carry a variety of air-to-air and air-to-ground missiles and bombs. It is also equipped with a 20-mm M61 Vulcan cannon. F/A-18s have flown reconnaissance, fighter escort, and air defense missions. In Afghanistan, these warplanes have been used to provide air support to ground troops in the form of airstrikes. They take off from U.S. Navy aircraft carriers in the North Arabian Sea.

UNMANNED AERIAL VEHICLES (UAVS)

UAVs, or drones, were being used in Afghanistan even before the events of 9/11. In 2000, drones were flying over areas of the country in search of Osama bin Laden and his al-Qaeda network. One of the most effective drones was the MQ-1 Predator. Outfitted with cameras and sensors, it was originally designed for reconnaissance and observation missions. It flew its first armed missions in the opening weeks of the Afghanistan war. Eventually, it became the United States' primary unmanned combat aircraft. The Predator, like all UAVs, is a remote-piloted aircraft operated by specialists at a ground control station. It is linked to this station by its own satellite system.

American Battles

Americans have been a leading force in the War in Afghanistan. They have been at the forefront of most battles and have played a key role in reducing the influence of the Taliban and insurgent forces. Many of the earlier battles in the conflict were powerful airstrikes that did massive damage to the country. The tougher battles have been those fought on the ground by both U.S. troops and their allies. These battles have required stealth, strategy, and quick thinking.

Chinook helicopters transported troops from the Bagram Air Base to the Shah-i-Kot valley in preparation for Operation Anaconda.

Operation Anaconda

Operation Anaconda was the first large-scale operation that involved conventional forces in direct battle. Led by the U.S. military, the operation included troops from several countries, including Australia, Canada, and Afghanistan. The goal of Operation Anaconda was to obliterate an insurgent stronghold in the Shah-i-Kot valley, in eastern Afghanistan.

The operation began on March 1, 2002, with U.S. and Afghan forces moving into the area to set up observation posts. The next day, the ISAF coalition forces began the actual attack. A **thermobaric** bomb was used to drive the insurgents from their cave hideouts. **Sniper** crews from the United States and Canada worked together to purge any insurgents they found, while air units began firing on the area.

MARCH 1

U.S. and Afghan forces move into the Shah-i-Kot valley to set up observation posts in preparation for the next day's attack.

MARCH 2

The United States and its ISAF allies begin the battle. Insurgents are bombed from their cave hideouts, while snipers and air units fire on any insurgents they find.

By the time helicopters brought them back to Bagram Air Base, the troops involved in Operation Anaconda had seized key terrain and taken several Taliban and al-Qaeda fighters prisoner.

The next day, more coalition forces joined the battle. There were now more than 1,500 coalition soldiers involved. They were met with strong resistance from Taliban and al-Qaeda fighters. Despite the direct counter-attack, the U.S. forces and their allies continued their advance. Over the next few days, they were able to surround the insurgents' cave compound.

Even when surrounded, the insurgents did not give up the fight. The battle continued for almost two more weeks. Ultimately, the coalition forces were able to destroy the insurgent stronghold and clear the area of Taliban and al-Qaeda fighters. The battle was declared officially over on March 18. While deaths on the coalition side were fewer than 20, it is estimated that the insurgents lost almost 300 fighters.

MARCH 3

More coalition troops are air dropped into the area to provide reinforcement. Within days, they are able to locate and surround the insurgents' cave compound.

MARCH 18

After holding the coalition forces at bay for almost two weeks, the insurgents are overcome. Coalition forces clear the area of enemy forces.

Battle of Wanat

On July 13, 2008, Taliban fighters attacked a remote outpost in the far eastern province of Nuristan. The outpost was located near the Pakistan border. It had been created to stem the flow of weapons into Afghanistan and was run primarily by U.S. Army soldiers. Like many such outposts, it was extremely vulnerable to enemy attack.

At 4:20 on the morning of July 13, Taliban forces launched rocket-propelled grenades and **mortars** at the small base. Rocket-propelled grenades hit the base's mortar pit, detonating U.S. ammunition and mortars. Other Taliban forces attacked the observation post situated just outside the base. Enemy fire hit the U.S. soldiers inside, stunning or injuring them all. While several soldiers tried to counter-attack with fire and grenades of their own, their force was seriously depleted because so many of them had been wounded or killed.

Wanat is located in Nuristan Province, an isolated area almost 125 miles (200 km) away from the Afghan capital. It remains extremely underdeveloped, with its citizens living in homes with few modern conveniences.

Support came from troops located in other observation posts. Some of the troops returned fire, while other soldiers dodged bullets and grenades to resupply the attacked observation post. After an hour of fighting, only one soldier remained alive at the observation post. Then, reinforcements finally arrived. Apache attack helicopters began an aerial assault on the Taliban forces. The Taliban fought the U.S. troops for several hours before retreating into the mountains.

JULY 12

Taliban fighters move into the remote village of Wanat and tell the locals to leave. They then move into position and prepare for attack.

JULY 13

At 4:20 am, Taliban forces begin launching grenades and mortars at the outpost. The initial attack detonates U.S. ammunition and mortars.

When the battle finally came to an end, nine U.S. soldiers lay dead. This death toll of U.S. soldiers was largest of any single battle since the start of the War in Afghanistan. The battle brought attention to other remote U.S. outposts that might be vulnerable to such surprise attacks. It was not long before steps were taken to improve the security and command at remote coalition outposts throughout Afghanistan.

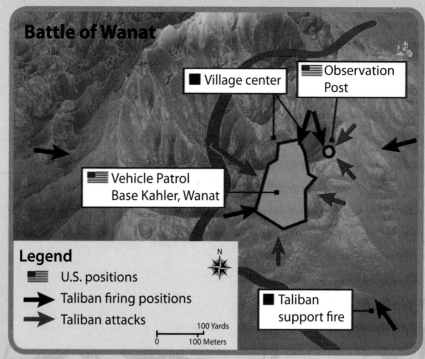

Battle of Wanat

■ Village center

■ Observation Post

■ Vehicle Patrol Base Kahler, Wanat

Legend

■ U.S. positions

➡ Taliban firing positions

➡ Taliban attacks

■ Taliban support fire

N

100 Yards
0   100 Meters

To build trust with the people of Nuristan, the United States government has announced plans to help modernize the province. Road construction projects are just one way the government hopes to befriend the local community.

JULY 13

While one group of Taliban fighters attack the outpost, another group attacks a nearby observation post. Several U.S. soldiers are either wounded or killed.

JULY 13

U.S. attack helicopters move in and begin firing on the Taliban forces. The fighting continues for several hours before the Taliban retreat and the battle comes to an end.

Operation Khanjar

In the early hours of July 2, 2009, the United States-led offensive known as Operation Khanjar began. Four thousand Marines joined with British and Afghan troops to move into the Taliban stronghold of the Helmand River valley, in southern Afghanistan. U.S. intelligence had indicated that the Taliban was using the area as a conduit for weapons and recruits. The troops were sent in to stop the Taliban's expansion in the area and restore the authority of the local government.

Shortly after midnight, the first group of Marines landed in desert fields just outside the town of Nawa-l-Barakzayi and began working their way toward the insurgents' location. The Marines and other members of the coalition forces then began carrying out raids on enemy compounds and chasing resistance fighters out of the region.

Operation Khanjar was the biggest offensive airlift by the Marines since the Vietnam War. It involved nearly 4,000 U.S. forces, as well as 650 Afghan police and soldiers.

JULY 2

U.S. Marines are joined by British and Afghan troops for an assault against Taliban forces in southern Afghanistan's Helmand River valley.

JULY 3

Taliban fighters hold off a Marine attack for eight hours before a U.S. attack helicopter bombs the Taliban compound, killing at least 30 of the fighters inside.

The raids had some success, but large-scale fighting was still necessary to eliminate the Taliban threat, especially in areas where the Taliban had been able to establish a base. On August 12, helicopters dropped a Marine **platoon** behind enemy lines in the Taliban-held town of Dahaneh. They fired their way into an insurgent compound, arresting the occupants and securing the building. Units of Marines then began entering the town, immediately encountering enemy fire.

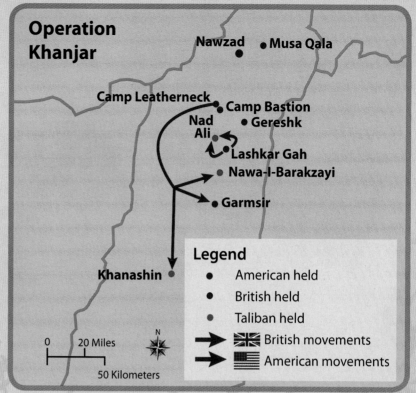

Operation Khanjar

Nawzad
Musa Qala
Camp Leatherneck
Camp Bastion
Nad Ali
Gereshk
Lashkar Gah
Nawa-I-Barakzayi
Garmsir
Khanashin

Legend
- American held
- British held
- Taliban held
→ 🇬🇧 British movements
→ 🇺🇸 American movements

0   20 Miles
50 Kilometers
N

A fierce battle began. The Marines made their way through the town, under heavy machine gun fire and rocket attacks. Their surface-to-surface missiles pounded the nearby hillsides where Taliban fighters were hiding. Finally, on August 16, the Marines were able to destroy the final Taliban compound and secure the town. Operation Khanjar came to its formal end within days. The success of this operation helped the Afghan government regain control of this part of Afghanistan.

AUGUST 12

Helicopters drop a platoon of Marines into the town of Daheneh, where they take over a Taliban compound. Other Marines enter the town, and a fierce battle ensues.

AUGUST 16

The Marines destroy the final Taliban compound in Daheneh and secure the town. As a result of this battle, the Taliban loses its stronghold in the area.

Heroic Americans

The men and women participating in the War in Afghanistan come from a range of backgrounds. They are united by a desire to fight for their country. While all perform heroic acts, as the war has progressed, some names have become better known than others. Some soldiers have been hailed for their bravery and strong leadership. Others have been celebrated because they performed feats unlike anyone else.

SAL GIUNTA
(1985-present)

Salvatore "Sal" Giunta is a former infantry soldier and staff sergeant who served with the U.S. Army from 2003 to 2011. In October of 2007, Sal was stationed in Afghanistan's Korengal Valley. On the evening of October 25, Sal was conducting a patrol with members of his platoon, when they were **ambushed** by insurgent fighters.

In seconds, several of Sal's comrades lay wounded on the ground. Sal, and a number of his company, began returning fire and throwing grenades to deter the enemy while they rescued the injured soldiers. When Sal realized that one of his unit was missing, he discovered that the enemy was dragging one of his best friends away. Sal engaged in fire with the enemy until they gave up the fight and retreated. While two members of the unit died in the attack, Sal saved his friend and played an instrumental role in bringing the skirmish to an end.

Sal was awarded the Medal of Honor for his efforts that evening. The Medal of Honor is the U.S. Armed Forces' highest decoration for valor. He was the first living person since the Vietnam War to receive this honor.

LEROY PETRY
(1979-present)

Leroy Petry is a Sergeant First Class with the U.S. Army. He enlisted in September of 1999 and became a member of the U.S. Army Rangers following basic training. The U.S. Army Rangers are a Special Forces Command unit.

On May 26, 2008, Leroy and his unit were assigned a rare daylight mission to capture a high-value enemy. Upon entering a courtyard, the Rangers came under fire. Leroy was shot in both legs but still managed to lead a team member to cover behind a chicken coop. Moments later, a grenade was lobbed at them. The explosion knocked everyone to the ground. A second grenade then landed next to the dazed soldiers. Leroy quickly picked up the grenade, planning to throw it before it detonated. However, it detonated as he was throwing it. The explosion blew off Leroy's right hand and covered him in **shrapnel**. Despite his grievous injury, Leroy was able to bandage his wrist while his comrades defeated the enemy. Leroy's heroic act saved the lives of his fellow Rangers. For his efforts that day, Leroy received the Medal of Honor.

MONICA BROWN
(1988-present)

Monica Brown is a medic serving with the U.S. Army. She is the first woman serving in Afghanistan and only the second woman since World War II to receive the Silver Star for bravery and valor in enemy action.

Monica was on a routine patrol aboard an armored personnel carrier during the early evening of April 25, 2007. Suddenly, an explosion boomed from behind. An improvised explosive device (IED) had exploded under one of the Humvees in the **convoy**. Enemy fire soon rained down on the convoy, but that did not stop Monica and her platoon sergeant from leaving their vehicle to help the people in the damaged Humvee. All five soldiers in the vehicle were injured, two critically. With bullets whizzing past her head, Monica worked with her comrades to move the injured soldiers to safety. Using her own body to provide cover, Monica began to administer medical attention to save her fellow soldiers' lives. Finally, she helped load her two patients into her vehicle and escape the fighting. Monica's fearless actions in the face of great danger saved the lives of both soldiers.

The Home Front

The 9/11 attacks and subsequent War in Afghanistan have had a profound effect on the United States. Following the attacks, the U.S. government began implementing new laws and created new government departments in order to strengthen the security of the country and its citizens. Some people have questioned the decisions made in this regard, but the federal government has remained firm in its resolve to reduce, and even eliminate, the terrorist threat.

The USA PATRIOT Act

On October 26, 2001, President Bush signed into law the USA PATRIOT Act. The act's acronym stands for Uniting (and) Strengthening America (by) Providing Appropriate Tools Required (to) Intercept (and) Obstruct Terrorism. The act was groundbreaking in that it granted law enforcement agencies more power than they had ever had to investigate suspected terrorist activity on U.S. soil. Authorities could use wiretaps to listen to private conversations. They could also regulate an individual's financial accounts and detain or deport any immigrants suspected of terrorism.

Many people saw these actions as infringements on their **civil liberties**. Individuals and organizations alike have taken the government to court over the invasion of privacy the act allows. The act underwent a review in 2006, and several changes were made to safeguard the U.S. Constitution and the rights of U.S citizens.

In the months leading up to the 2006 review, citizens across the country led protests against the USA PATRIOT Act.

President Bush signed the Homeland Security Act on November 25, 2002, in the East Room of the White House. Several members of Congress joined him to show their support for the act.

The Department of Homeland Security

In November 2002, President George W. Bush announced the establishment of the United States Department of Homeland Security (DHS). While the Department of Defense is in charge of military actions abroad, the DHS concentrates on efforts to protect the United States from within. The department's main focus is to keep the country safe from terrorist attacks. However, it is also responsible for handling natural disasters. As part of its mandate, the DHS took over responsibility of both the Immigration and Customs Enforcement agency and Citizenship and Immigration Services, and was given authority over departments that dealt with border patrol and U.S. customs.

9/11 Commission

The National Commission on Terrorist Attacks Upon the United States was established on November 27, 2002. It sought to create a "full and complete account of the circumstances surrounding the September 11 attacks" and a plan to respond to them.

The 9/11 Commission's final report was made available in bookstores throughout the country. It became a bestseller as people tried to find reasons for the 9/11 attacks.

The commission was made up of five Democrats and five Republicans. It was chaired by former New Jersey Governor Thomas Kean. The commission's first hearings were held on March 31, 2003. Government officials called to testify included former Secretary of State Colin Powell, Secretary of Defense Donald Rumsfeld, and even President Bush himself. The commission issued its final report on July 22, 2004. It concluded that several errors were made by the CIA and the Federal Bureau of Investigation (FBI). These errors allowed the 9/11 terrorists to avoid detection and follow through with their plan.

Following its investigation into the events of September 11, the commission provided recommendations on how to guard against future attacks. It suggested that the United States help Afghanistan rebuild and support other Muslim countries in their struggles to be free of tyrannical governments.

Donald Rumsfeld, along with Joint Chiefs of Staff Chairman General Richard B. Myers, were two of the first people to speak before the 9/11 Commission.

Protests

The decision to wage war in Afghanistan was not popular with all Americans. Many felt the United States should wait until other countries joined the fight. Others felt it was unjust to invade a foreign country. .

These anti-war sentiments led to nationwide protests. One of the first occurred on September 29, 2001, when 20,000 people gathered in Washington, D.C. to protest the government's plans to invade Afghanistan. A week later, another 10,000 protestors marched to Union Square in New York City on October 7, 2001, just as U.S. troops were beginning their assault on Taliban targets in Afghanistan. In April the following year, another protest was held in Washington. More than 75,000 people participated in a protest against the war in Afghanistan.

U.S. citizens have not been alone in their anti-war protests. Other countries, including Germany, have held demonstrations demanding the withdrawal of their troops from Afghanistan.

Over time, the focus of the protests changed. The loss of lives and the lack of headway in Afghanistan led people in the United States and other countries to question their participation in the war. They began campaigning and demonstrating to bring their troops home.

Many of the people who protested against the war felt that the cost of the war was going to be excessive and that the money would be better spent on domestic problems.

The Conflict Continues

By July 2009, the ISAF had about 64,500 troops in Afghanistan. Approximately 30,000 of them were American. However, by September, the Taliban was making at least one insurgent attack per week in about 80 percent of the country. There were concerns within the ISAF that its forces were losing ground in the war and that defeating Taliban forces may not be possible without more troops.

On December 1, 2009, President Obama announced that he would send an additional 30,000 soldiers to Afghanistan over a period of six months, but proposed to begin troop withdrawals 18 months from that date. However, the president of Afghanistan, Hamid Karzai, wanted U.S. military support for another 15 to 20 years. Ultimately, the U.S. sent almost 100,000 troops in total to Afghanistan and extended its combat mission there until 2014.

Hamid Karzai has made several visits to the United States since the war began. One such visit occurred in 2009, shortly before President Obama announced that the U.S. was sending more troops to Afghanistan.

Most Pakistanis were unaware that Osama bin Laden was living in their midst. Many gathered outside bin Laden's compound after his death was announced.

While the military mission continued in Afghanistan, the United States also kept searching for Osama bin Laden, the mastermind behind the 9/11 attacks. Initially believed to be in Afghanistan, by 2010, U.S. intelligence received reports that bin Laden was living in a compound in the neighboring country of Pakistan. The CIA began surveillance of the compound to confirm that the terrorist leader was there. By January 2011, the CIA felt confident that the compound was Osama bin Laden's home base. In the early hours of May 2, 2011, U.S. military helicopters dropped more than 20 Navy SEALs into the compound. The SEALs quickly located bin Laden and brought him to his death. Even though the mission was a success, it did not bring an end to al-Qaeda. The terrorist group continues to present a threat to Afghanistan, the United States, and the world.

The War in Afghanistan has proven to be a great challenge to the United States and its allied forces. The coalition forces have suffered significant loss of life. Many other troops have returned home with life-altering injuries. Afghanistan itself has lost thousands of **civilians** and troops to the fighting. When the losses are compared to the achievements, it is difficult to gauge the success of the war. Even though the Taliban has been removed from power, it is still a strong presence in Afghanistan, undermining the efforts of the country's current government.

The Aftermath

Even though the War in Afghanistan continues, the United States is taking steps to reduce its military contribution in the next few years. The emphasis on military action is shifting toward reconstruction efforts. This means that U.S. military and civilian personnel will be helping Afghanistan build new infrastructure so that it can govern, defend, and even modernize itself.

Paying a Price

One of the main concerns many Americans have had about the extended U.S. participation in the war is the human cost. As the war intensified, the United States saw more and more lives lost, both military and civilian. In the face of this growing death toll, some Americans questioned the validity of the war and the United States' role in it.

The growing financial cost of the war has also come under scrutiny. In 2013, estimates put the cost to U.S. taxpayers as high as $641.7 billion. Some of this money went to humanitarian aid and veterans' benefits, but the bulk of it has been attributed to the military effort itself. People have argued that the money could have been better spent in the United States, helping U.S. citizens directly.

Military funerals have become a regular occurrence as a result of the War in Afghanistan.

Rebuilding Afghanistan

The U.S. government is very aware that war has had a negative impact on the Afghan people and economy. The government has created programs to help Afghanistan rebuild. Much of this work is being done by Provincial Reconstruction Teams (PRTs). Consisting of military and civilian personnel, these teams work with both the government and citizens of Afghanistan.

PRT members work closely with the people of Afghanistan to improve their quality of life.

Afghanistan is a developing country. Most of its citizens live in rural communities and rely on agriculture for their survival. Living conditions are poor for most of the population. PRT agencies work with these people to help them develop sustainable farming techniques and sell their products. The PRTs also help the Afghanistan government create strategies to help overcome regional differences. This will help the government have a stronger national presence and reduce the influence of the country's insurgent forces.

Troop Withdrawal

The United States has taken a leading role in the War on Afghanistan since it began. However, the U.S. government has always been aware that its military contribution cannot go on forever. In order to ensure a smooth transition when their forces leave, the U.S. government and military have been training Afghan troops to assume control of their own national defense. Over the past few years, the U.S. government has monitored the ability of Afghanistan to defend itself, waiting for the right time to begin a permanent withdrawal of combat troops.

In June 2011, President Obama announced the plan for a gradual withdrawal of troops from Afghanistan. By the end of 2012, troops had been reduced from 100,000 to 67,000. The U.S. government's plan is to have all combat troops return home by the end of 2014. After that, some U.S. forces may remain to train and advise Afghan police and military.

By The Numbers

U.S. Casualties

Casualties refer to soldiers who have been either wounded or killed during the war. Not all casualties happen as a result of battle. The chart to the right indicates how many Americans have been wounded or killed in each year of the war.

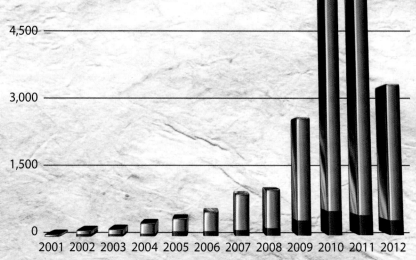

Americans killed in Afghanistan **Americans wounded in Afghanistan**

6,000

4,500

3,000

1,500

0

2001 2002 2003 2004 2005 2006 2007 2008 2009 2010 2011 2012

Duration of U.S. Wars

The War in Afghanistan has surpassed the Vietnam War as the longest war the United States has fought. As of January 2013, American troops have been fighting in Afghanistan for 136 months. The following chart compares the duration of the War in Afghanistan to other U.S. conflicts.

Months

War	Months
War in Afghanistan	136
Iraq War	106
Gulf War	2
Vietnam	129
Korean War	37
World War II	46
World War I	24
Spanish American War	10
Civil War	52
Mexican-American War	22
War of 1812	32
American Revolutionary War	96

Reconstruction Spending

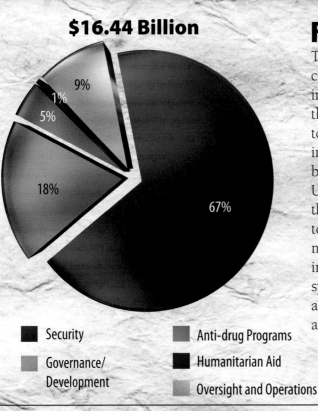

$16.44 Billion

- Security — 67%
- Governance/Development — 18%
- Anti-drug Programs — 5%
- Humanitarian Aid — 1%
- Oversight and Operations — 9%

The United States government has contributed to reconstruction efforts in Afghanistan since the early years of the war. However, the funding targeted toward these programs has increased in recent years as the United States begins preparing Afghanistan for the U.S. withdrawal. This chart indicates the funding that the United States put toward reconstruction in 2012. While much of this money was directed toward improving security and government systems, some funding was also allocated to humanitarian aid and anti-drug programs.

Cost of the War in Afghanistan

Supporting the American mission in Afghanistan has cost the country's government greatly. This chart provides spending estimates for each year of the war.

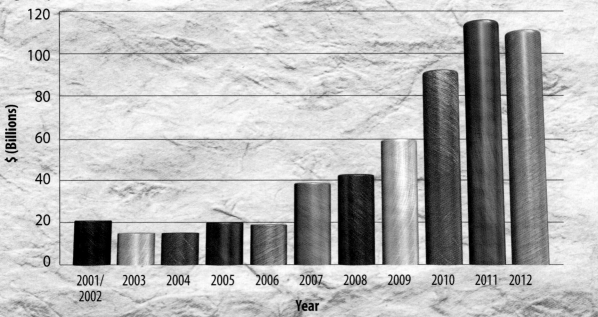

$ (Billions)

Year

War Casualties

Coalition forces have suffered more than 3,200 deaths as a result of the War in Afghanistan. For the first five years, the majority of these casualties were U.S. forces. Other countries, including the United Kingdom, have sustained higher casualties as they took responsibility of highly dangerous regions such as Helmand and Kandahar. For many countries, these are the first war casualties they have experienced since the end of World War II.

This chart shows the losses suffered by many of the coalition countries that have participated in the war.

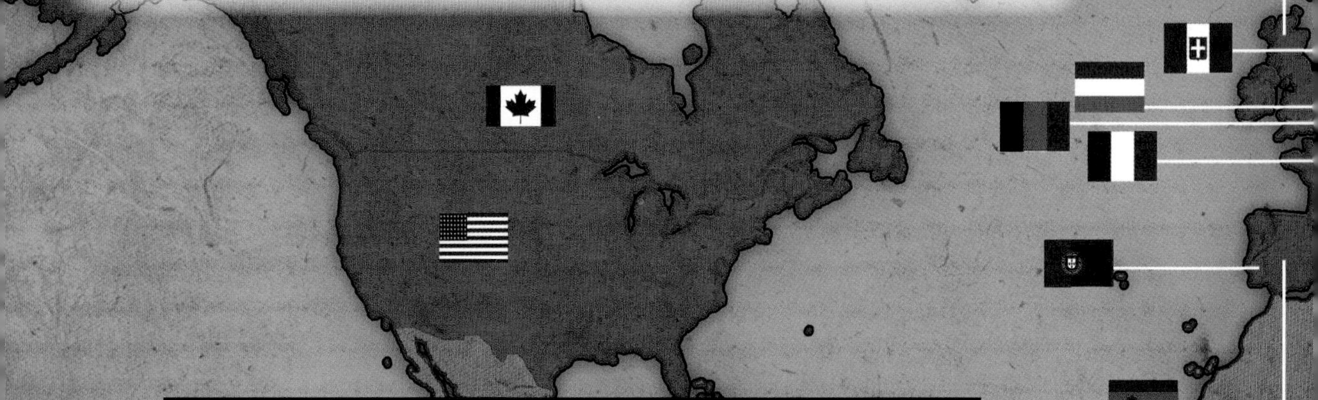

Fatalities By Country

Country	Total	Country	Total
Australia	39	Lithuania	1
Belgium	1	Netherlands	25
Canada	158	New Zealand	11
Czech Republic	5	Norway	10
Denmark	43	Poland	36
Estonia	9	Portugal	2
Finland	2	Romania	19
France	86	South Korea	1
Georgia	20	Spain	34
Germany	54	Sweden	5
Hungary	7	Turkey	14
Italy	47	United Kingdom	444
Jordan	2	United States	2,227
Latvia	3		

Total 3,285

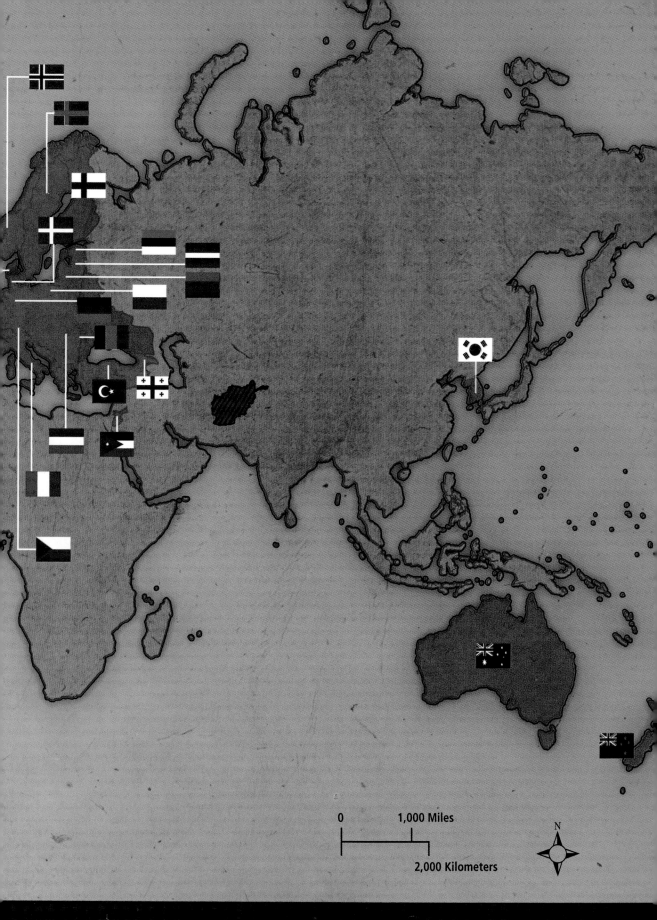

How We Remember

As of January 2013, the United States has lost more than 2,000 soldiers in the War in Afghanistan. Many others have been seriously injured. The ongoing conflict has affected Americans all over the country. People want to honor the wounded, the dead, and those who continue to fight the war against terrorism.

AMERICA'S RESPONSE MONUMENT

An impressive 16-foot (4.88-m) tall bronze statue stands in the lobby of the One World Financial Center opposite the site of the former twin towers in New York City. America's Response Monument is dedicated to the United States Special Forces troops, who were the first U.S. troops to enter Afghanistan in October 2001. The sculpture depicts a Special Forces soldier riding a horse. It is based on a photo taken just after military operations began in Afghanistan. A Special Operations team named Task Force Dagger rode on horseback with Northern Alliance troops as they advanced on Taliban targets.

AFGHAN-IRAQ FREEDOM MEMORIAL

The first memorial dedicated to soldiers killed in the War in Afghanistan was the Afghan-Iraq Freedom Memorial in Salem, Oregon. The focal point of the memorial is the bronze statue of a soldier kneeling down to offer a helping hand. He sits atop a pedestal that overlooks a large pool of water. At the bottom of the pool is a map of the world. Across the pool from the soldier is a plaque bearing the names of those soldiers from the state of Oregon who have given their lives in the wars in Iraq and Afghanistan. Surrounding the pool are the flags of the branches of the U.S. military.

MONTANA FALLEN SOLDIER MEMORIAL

In April 2013, a sculpture at the University of Montana became the state's official tribute to those who died during the Iraq and Afghanistan wars. The sculpture features a family of four standing before a soldier's rifle, helmet, and boots. The figures are surrounded by 50 granite markers. Each marker has been designed to hold the name, rank, branch of service, and hometown of a Montana soldier who died in either the Iraq or Afghanistan War. The Fallen Soldier Memorial stands near Memorial Row, a grove of trees planted to commemorate the soldiers who died in World War I.

Americans have found unique ways to honor these individuals. While traditional memorials have been built to honor the fallen troops, other memorials have been created from spontaneous outpourings of thanks and remembrance. These memorials have created a bond among Americans from one coast to the other.

VETERANS WAR MEMORIAL OF TEXAS

The Veterans War Memorial of Texas was built to honor the 1.4 million American military personnel missing in action during the nation's wars and conflicts beginning in 1775. The memorial covers an area of 5 acres (2 hectares) in McAllen, Texas. It is divided into five sections. Each section has a set of granite panels that tells the story of one of the conflicts. The War in Afghanistan is part of the All Wars section. Four panels pay tribute to the sacrifices several local soldiers and their families made in the war against terrorism. The Memorial Complex features sculptures and pathways inscribed with people's names.

THE YELLOW RIBBON

Ribbons have been used to show support for U.S. troops fighting around the world for many years. During the Gulf War of the early 1990s, Americans began tying yellow ribbons around trees. These ribbons were meant to show **solidarity** with the troops fighting overseas. The yellow ribbon tradition continued in 2003 when America invaded Iraq. Various ribbons are used today to show support for U.S. troops. While there are plenty of yellow ribbons, camouflage ribbons are also very popular. Some people wear a red, white, and blue ribbon as a symbol of their patriotism.

MEMORIAL DAY

Memorial Day is a federal holiday that is observed on the final Monday of May each year. It is a day to remember those who died while serving their country in the U.S. Armed Forces. The first Memorial Day was held after the American Civil War to commemorate those who died on both sides of the war. Today, people use this day to visit cemeteries and memorials, placing flags and other tokens of remembrance. Many cities hold parades with veterans from various wars marching or riding in military vehicles. There are also solemn ceremonies, such as those at Arlington National Cemetery in Virginia.

Test Yourself

MIX 'n MATCH

1. President George W. Bush
2. Infantry
3. President Barack Obama
4. Hamid Karzai
5. Special Forces
6. PRTs
7. ISAF

a. Troop withdrawal
b. Rebuilding Afghanistan
c. Face-to-face combat
d. United Nations
e. Green Berets
f. War on Terror
g. Afghanistan president

TRUE OR FALSE

1. The War in Afghanistan is the longest war America has been involved in.

2. When the United States took action against the Taliban in Afghanistan, its main allies were Australia, Canada, France, and the United Kingdom.

3. The United States operates the largest navy in the world.

4. The first phase of the War in Afghanistan began on October 11, 2001.

5. Night vision devices can be snapped on to the front of a soldier's Advanced Combat Helmet.

6. U.S. Marines operated alongside British and Afghan forces in Operation Khanjar.

7. The Department of Homeland Security is responsible for anti-terrorism operations overseas.

8. The U.S. government has vowed to withdraw all combat troops from Afghanistan by the end of 2014.

MULTIPLE CHOICE

1. What name did the U.S. government give to the War in Afghanistan?
   a. Operation Anaconda
   b. Operation Enduring Freedom
   c. The War on Tyranny
   d. Operation Fighting Eagle

2. In which year did Soviet Union invade Afghanistan?
   a. 1977
   b. 1978
   c. 1979
   d. 1980

3. Approximately how many countries have joined the war in Afghanistan?
   a. 40
   b. 50
   c. 60
   d. 85

4. What kind of group did the United States form with other allied countries?
   a. An alliance
   b. A union
   c. A coalition
   d. A commission

5. During the first hours of the War in Afghanistan, from where were Tomahawk missiles launched?
   a. U.S. Navy destroyers and cruisers
   b. F/A Hornet fighter/bombers
   c. Ground-to ground platforms
   d. The surrounding mountainsides

6. How much might a soldier's Improved Outer Tactical Vest weigh?
   a. 30 pounds
   b. 35 pounds
   c. 45 pounds
   d. 50 pounds

7. What was the first large scale operation of conventional troops in the War in Afghanistan?
   a. Operation Thunderbird
   b. Operation Enduring Freedom
   c. Operation Chinook
   d. Operation Anaconda

Key Words

ally: a person or group who is associated with another for a common purpose

ambushed: staged a surprise attack

amphibious: on both land and water

ballistic: relating to the flight of projectiles

civilians: people who are not members of the military

civil liberties: the freedom of citizens to exercise certain basic rights without government interference

close quarters combat: fighting that engages the enemy at short range

colonial rule: relating to colonies, or areas that remain under the control of another country

communist: in theory, a system where all people enjoy equal social and economic status

convoy: a group of vehicles traveling together

democratically: in a way that supports social equality

dictators: people who rule absolutely and oppressively

guerrilla: an irregular armed force that is usually politically motivated

infrastructure: the foundation for an organization or system

insurgent: a person who takes part in an uprising

jihad: a holy war undertaken by Muslims

logistics: planning for the movement of troops and equipment

mortars: short-barreled cannons

platoon: a subdivision of a company of troops

reconnaissance: the process of obtaining information about the position of the enemy

shrapnel: fragments from artillery fire

sniper: someone who shoots at targets from a concealed area

solidarity: unity in sympathies and interests

Soviet: belonging to the Soviet Union, a former federal union of 15 constituent republics in Eurasia

Taliban: a fundamentalist Islamic group that controlled Afghanistan in the early 2000s

thermobaric: a bomb containing explosive gas

Index

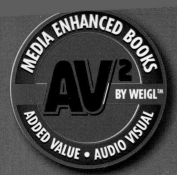

Log on to www.av2books.com

AV² by Weigl brings you media enhanced books that support active learning. Go to www.av2books.com, and enter the special code found on page 2 of this book. You will gain access to enriched and enhanced content that supplements and complements this book. Content includes video, audio, weblinks, quizzes, a slide show, and activities.

AV² Online Navigation

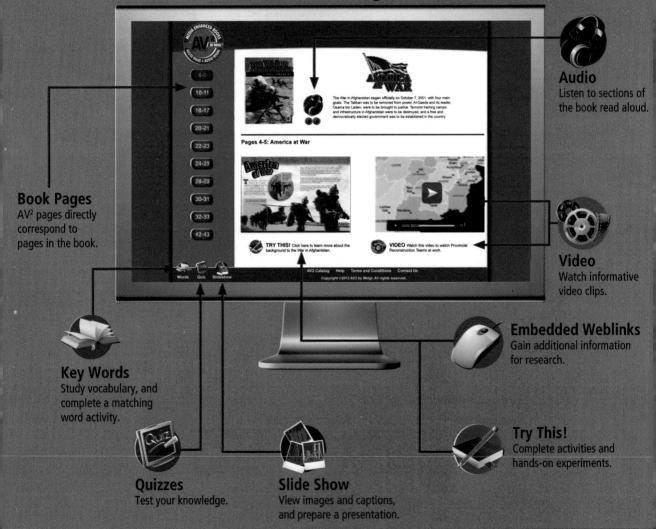

Audio
Listen to sections of the book read aloud.

Book Pages
AV² pages directly correspond to pages in the book.

Video
Watch informative video clips.

Key Words
Study vocabulary, and complete a matching word activity.

Embedded Weblinks
Gain additional information for research.

Try This!
Complete activities and hands-on experiments.

Quizzes
Test your knowledge.

Slide Show
View images and captions, and prepare a presentation.

AV² was built to bridge the gap between print and digital. We encourage you to tell us what you like and what you want to see in the future.

Sign up to be an AV² Ambassador at www.av2books.com/ambassador.